Valentine's Day Coloring

100 Coloring Pages

Hannah Knight

First Published, 2020

Printed in the United States of America

www.hannahlynnknight.weebly.com

@hannah.knight02221997 on Facebook

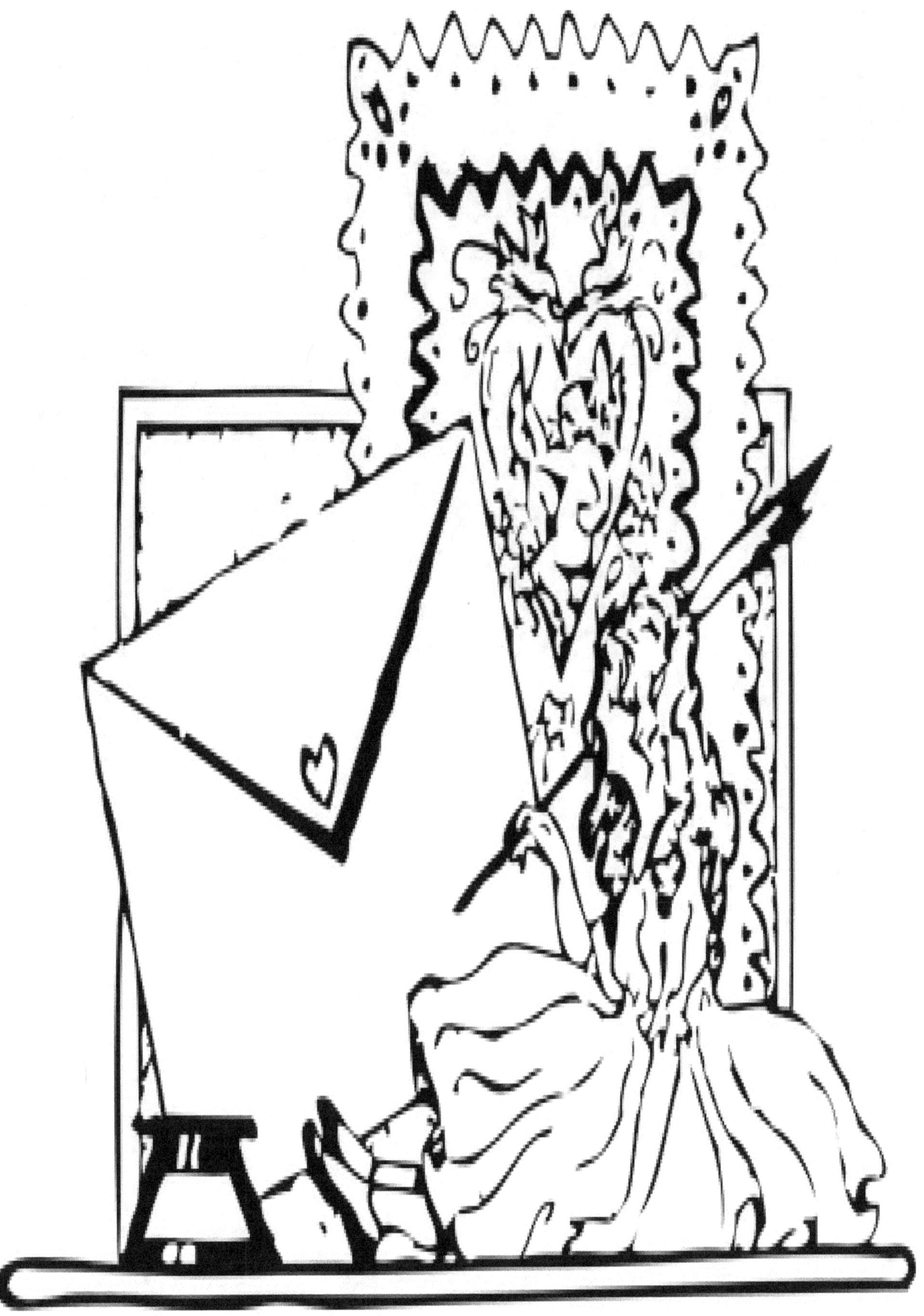

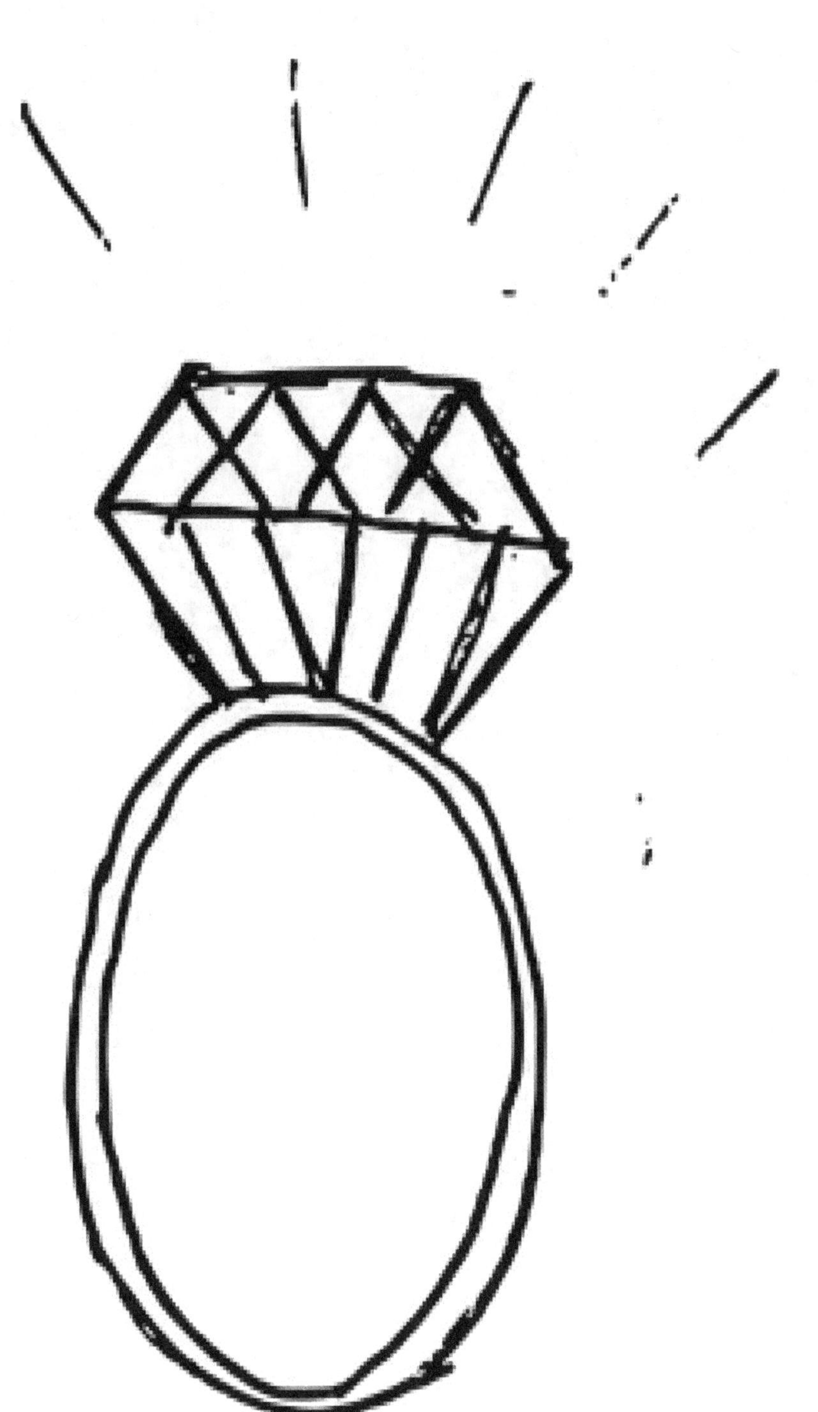

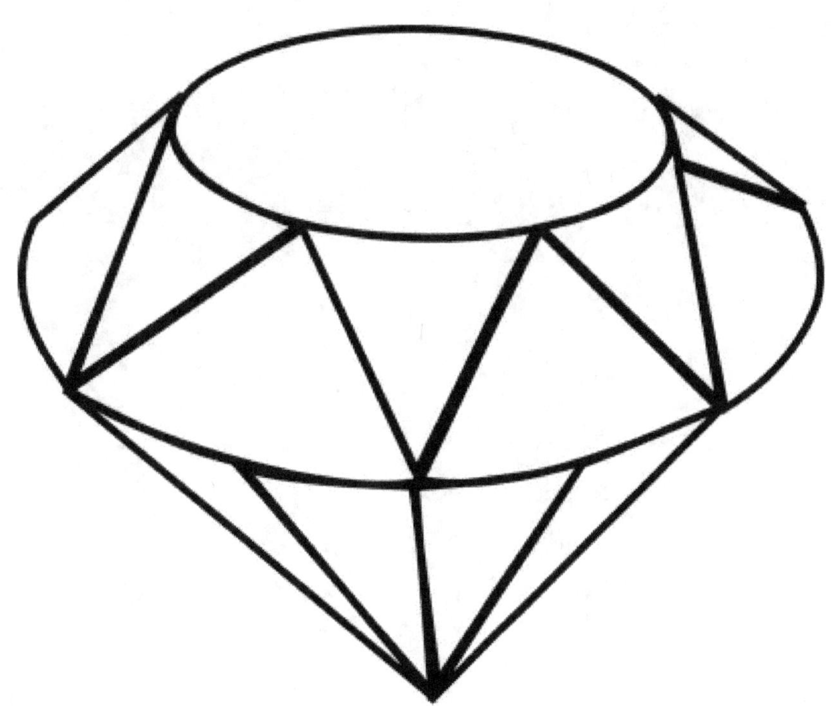

I LOVE YOU

Love

Happy
Valentine's
Day

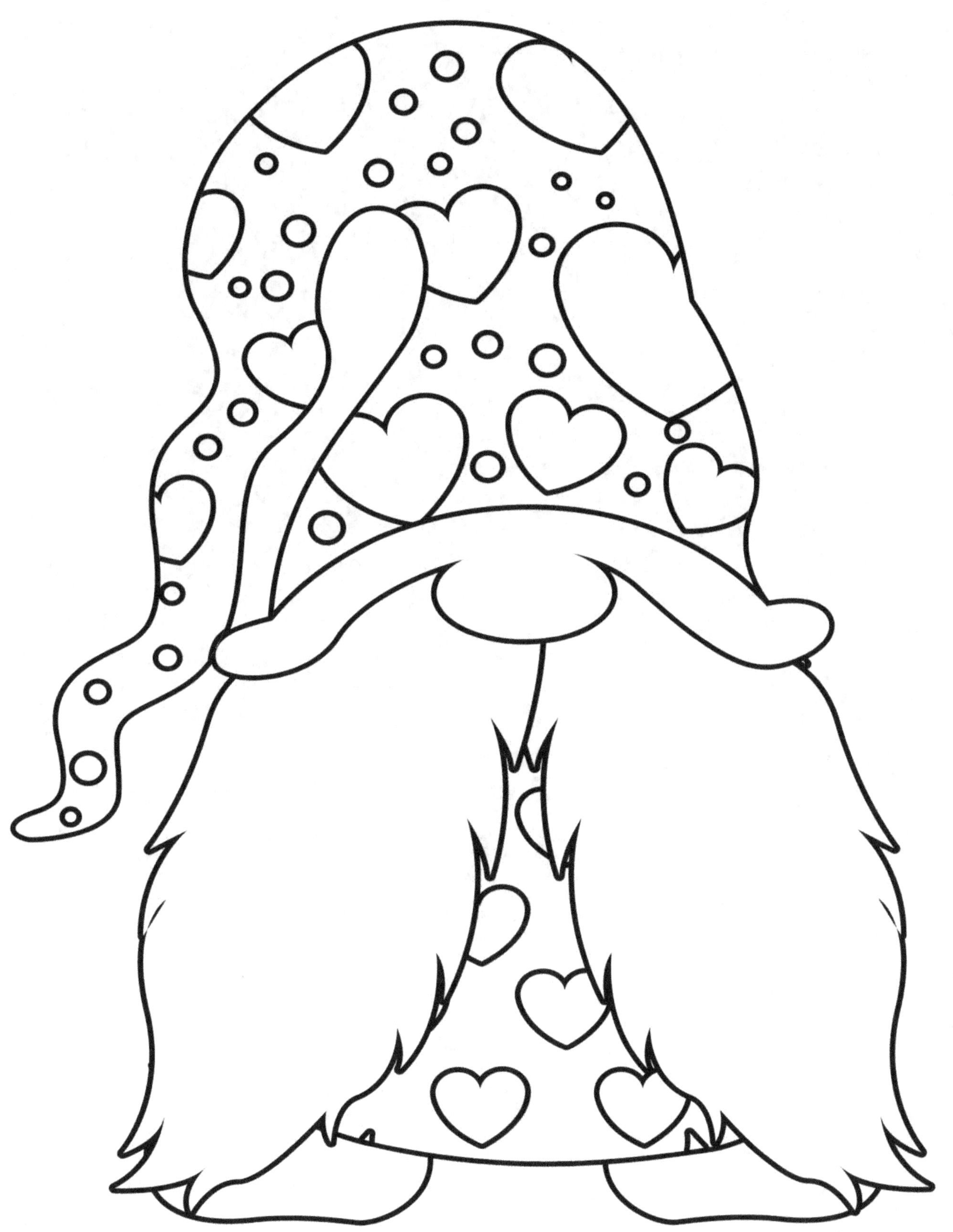

Be My
Galentine!

Be
Happy
Be
Bright
Be you!

You are a beautiful tropical fish

Smart as a whip, and cool under pressure.

You're a genius!

Your brain is almost as
perfect as your face.

You
are
LOVED

You are a beautiful, sassy
mannequin come to life...

You Have ALL the Strengths

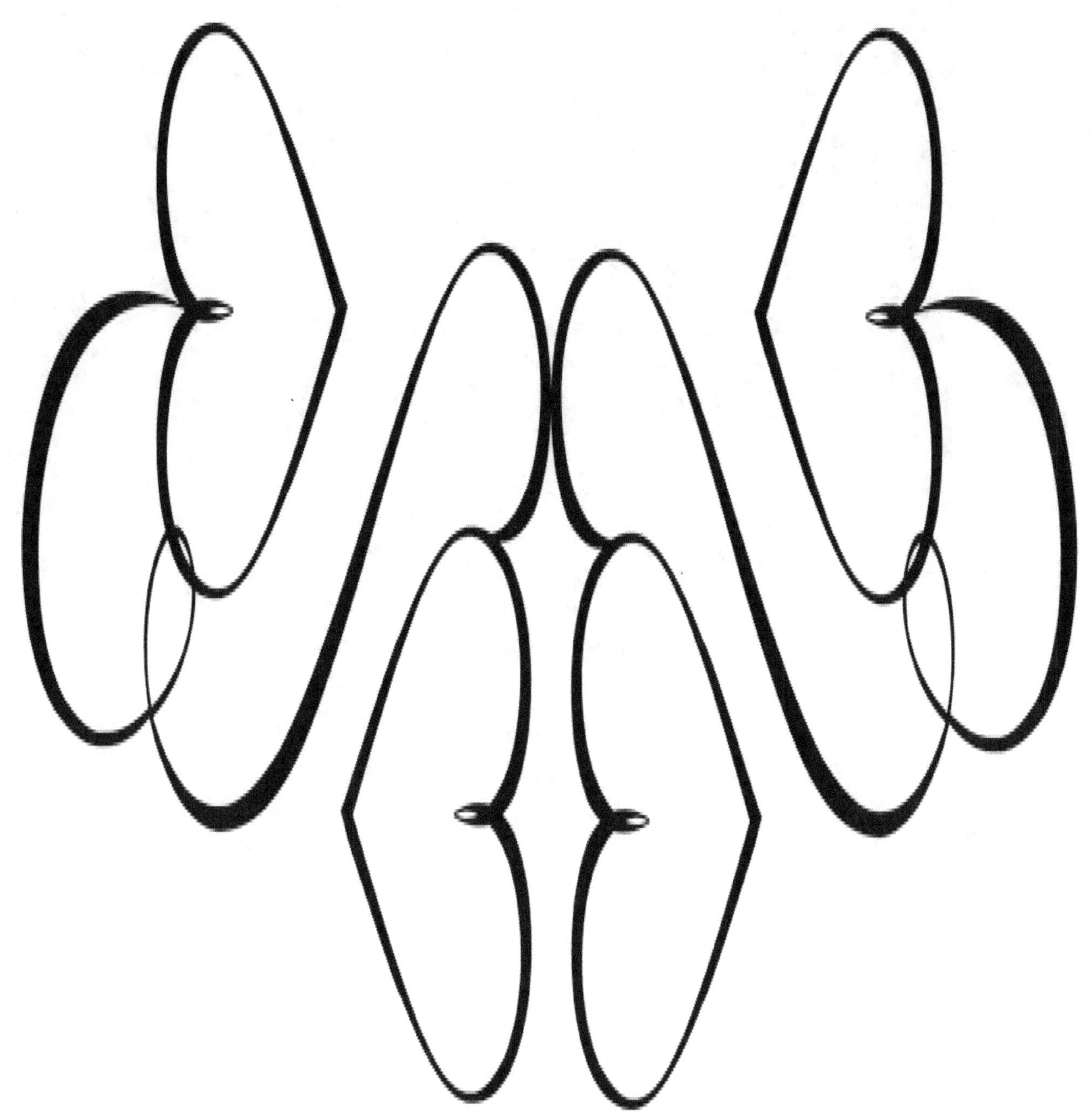

LIFE
LIFE
LIFE
LIFE

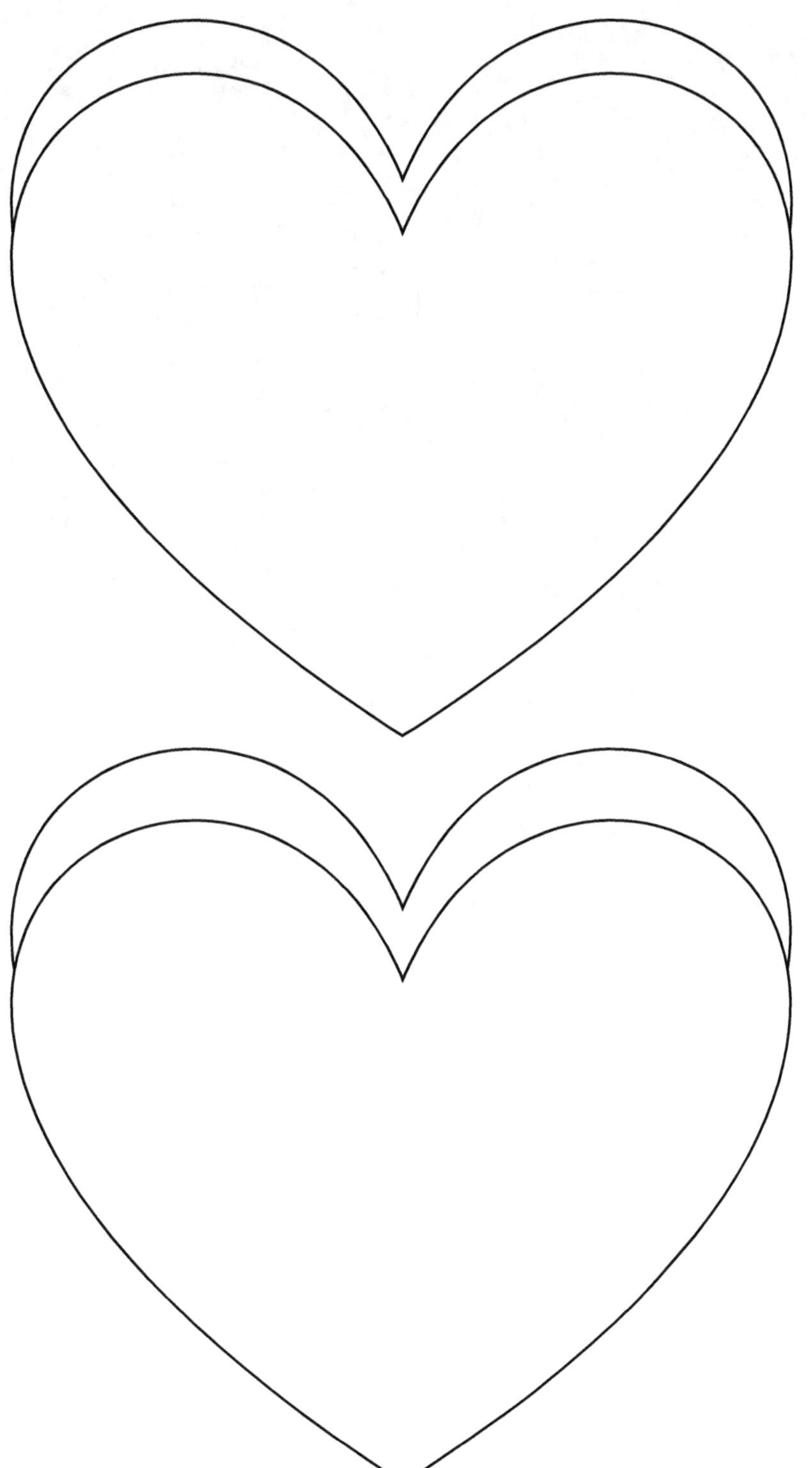

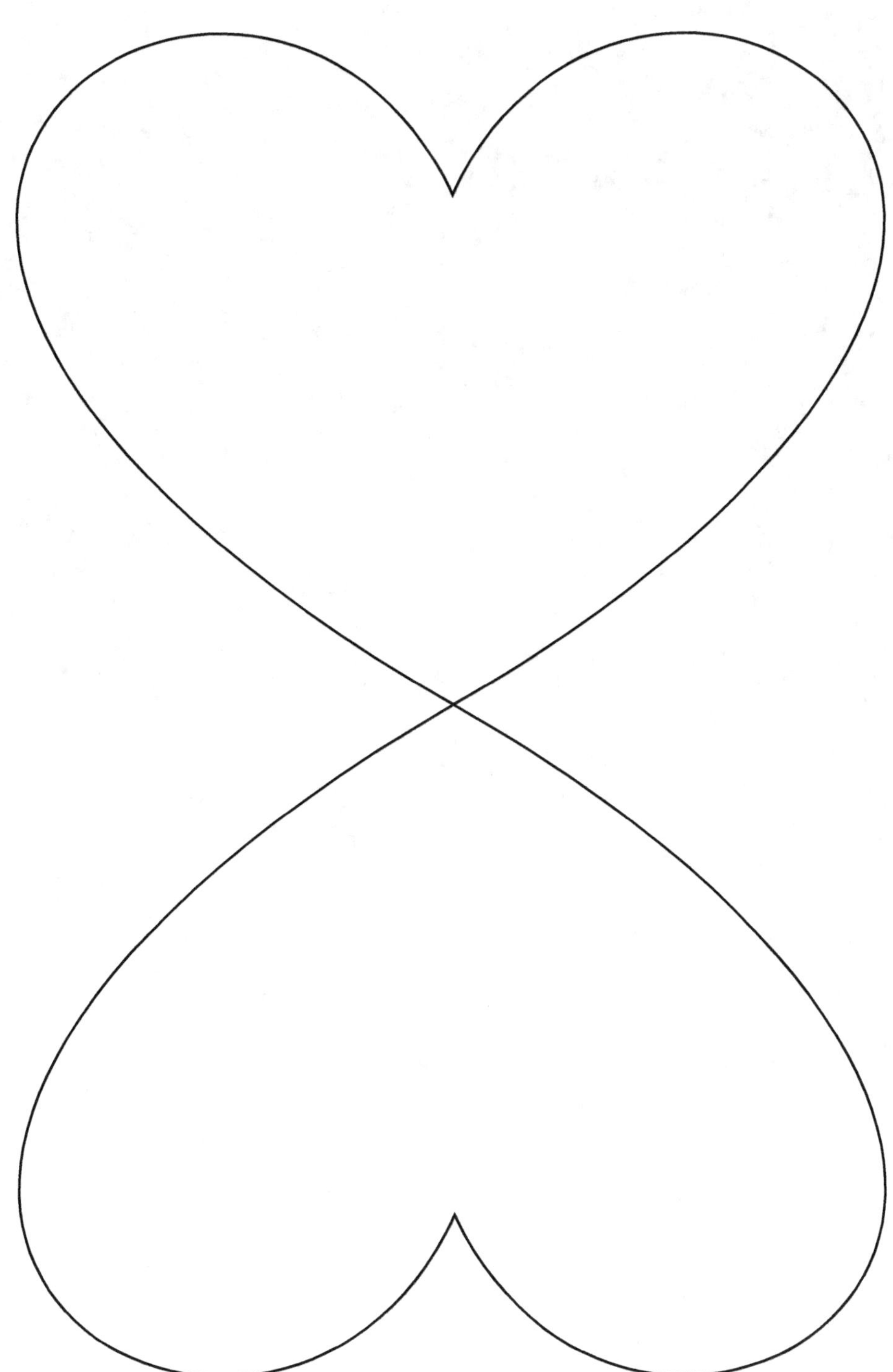

www.ingramcontent.com/pod-product-compliance
Lightning Source LLC
Chambersburg PA
CBHW080901160726
48000CB00009B/2813